Taking Stock

The World of Business

by Neale S. Godfrey

Illustrated by Randy Verougstraete

Modern Curriculum Press
Parsippany, New Jersey

To Granny Jewel—my best friend, my strength, my biggest supporter
(who always says I look good on TV), and who happens to be my grandma.
Love, Neale

Editorial assistance provided by Pubworks, Inc.
Design: Rosanne Guarara

All photographs by Silver Burdett Ginn (SBG) unless otherwise noted.

4: t. © Carl Purcell/Photo Researchers, Inc. 6: t.,m.,b. Courtesy, Ben & Jerry's. 13: UPI/Corbis-Bettmann. 15: t. © 1998 Al Stephenson/Woodfin Camp & Associates. 17: Winfield I. Parks/© National Geographic Image Collection. 25: t. Robert Brenner/PhotoEdit. 30–31: Denise DeLuise/First Image West, Inc. 35: top to bottom Bryan Peterson/The Stock Market; Jeremy Hardie/Tony Stone Images; © Phillip Hayson/Photo Researchers, Inc.; Peter Pearson/Tony Stone Images.

Acknowledgement: Modern Curriculum Press, Inc. gratefully acknowledges the following for the use of copyrighted material: Stock Quotations Table. Reprinted by permission of The Wall Street Journal, ©1997. All Rights Reserved Worldwide.

Modern Curriculum Press
An Imprint of Pearson Learning
299 Jefferson Road
Parsippany, NJ 07054

1 2 3 4 5 6 7 8 9 10 CA 06 05 04 03 02 01 00 99

A Note to Kids

What do you need to know about money? There are coins, there are bills. You see things, you buy things. Simple, right? Not so fast. When it comes to money, things can get pretty complicated. Money involves more than just dollars and cents. There are consumers and producers, supply and demand, recession and depression, taxes and foreign exchange, stocks and bonds. That's quite a mouthful. And that's only the beginning!

Welcome to *Taking Stock: The World of Business*. In this book you'll learn about lots of things that involve money. You'll learn what an economy is and how it works. You'll learn what role the government plays in keeping the economy rolling. You'll also learn about investing money and the stock market. You will see that when it comes to investing money you have many choices.

Taking Stock: The World of Business will help you to discover how much fun understanding the economy can be and how worthwhile the knowledge is!

Neale S. Godfrey

Contents

Chapter 1

The Big Picture of Money— The Economy!

What **is** it?
What does it **mean** to **you**?

ECONOMY. It's a big word. Everyone, from your family to the President, talks about it.

How does the economy work?
What is supply and demand?
What are inflation and recession?

This chapter will help you understand some of the big issues surrounding money. You'll see what it takes to start a business. You'll explore the relationships between buyers and sellers, prices and quantity—and more. When you've finished the chapter, you'll have a better idea about the big picture—the big picture of money, that is.

It's the Economy

Consumers and Producers

From the moment you spend your first dime, you are a **consumer**—someone who exchanges money for goods or services. It doesn't take much training or preparation to be a consumer. In fact, most people get into the habit of spending more easily than they do saving. Are you a saver, a spender, or both?

As a spender or consumer, you are faced with many choices—often very tempting ones. But it's your job to use your money wisely. You could say it's a full-time job. But there's another side to being a consumer. Most consumers are **producers** as well. Through work as individuals or as part of a company, people help produce all the goods and services that consumers use. The **economy** is how consumers and producers work together to produce and use all the things people want and need. An economy includes people, natural resources, and all the things people produce and consume.

Big, Bigger, Biggest

How well consumers and producers work together is one measure of how well the economy is doing. But a person can be involved in more than one economy. How can that be? A town or a state has a local economy, which is made up of the consumers and producers in that town or state. A country has a national economy, which is made up of all the consumers and producers from all parts of that country. An international economy is made up of the different goods and services produced and consumed by many different countries. Did you realize that you are a part of all these economies?

Word Bank

consumer *someone who buys and uses goods and services*

producer *the person or business that provides goods and services*

economy *the way in which human resources and natural resources are used to produce goods and services*

A Matter of Fact

The world economy includes the least populated country, Nauru (a small island near Australia with a population of about 10,000), as well as China, the most populated country in the world (with over 1 billion people). Altogether, the world economy is made up of almost 6 billion people!

2

A Sector Here, A Sector There

An economy is made up of different types of workers. Think of the adults in your family. What kind of work do they do? Some people work in the **private sector**, which means they work for themselves or for a company or business.

Did you know that the government is also an **employer**? The government hires people to run its offices and services. The government uses some of the money it collects from taxes to pay the salaries of these workers. People who work for the government work in the **public sector** of the economy.

A Penny for Your Thoughts

Suppose that you live in a town on the coast. You have a friend who lives in a town in the mountains. What types of jobs might be available in your town but not in your friend's town? What jobs might be found in both?

It's Only Natural

Think about the area you live in. What types of jobs are available near you? Why do you think people in your area do the jobs they do? People's jobs have a lot to do with where they live. The geography and **natural resources** of a particular region often determine the kind of work that is available in that area. Natural resources such as oil or iron ore often determine related jobs and industries, such as mining and steel production.

Word Bank

private sector *the part of the economy produced by individuals and businesses*

employer *a person or company for whom other people work for pay*

public sector *the part of the economy produced by the government*

natural resource *a supply of something that is found naturally on Earth*

3

What's in a Business?

You are part of the national economy. You use goods and services, so you are a consumer. But how can you be a producer? You can by running or being part of a **business**. A business brings in money by selling goods or services. There are two basic types of businesses. A manufacturing business, like an in-line skate factory, makes and sells a product. In a service business, such as dry cleaning or home construction, someone does work in exchange for money or goods. What types of businesses have you been involved in?

It's **Not** Just **Busy**-ness

Have you ever started your own business? If so, you are an **entrepreneur**. An entrepreneur is someone who creates a business and often hires workers to help him or her. An entrepreneur makes the best use of natural resources as well as the talents and energies of workers to try to create a successful business.

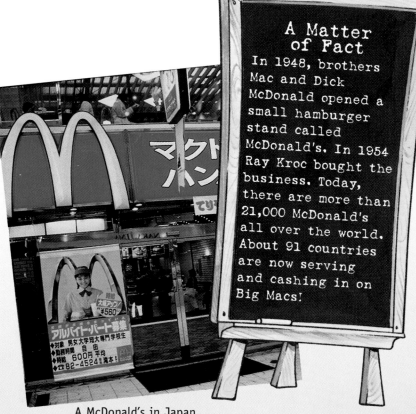

A McDonald's in Japan

A Matter of Fact

In 1948, brothers Mac and Dick McDonald opened a small hamburger stand called McDonald's. In 1954 Ray Kroc bought the business. Today, there are more than 21,000 McDonald's all over the world. About 91 countries are now serving and cashing in on Big Macs!

Word Bank

business *an enterprise that brings in money from selling goods or services*

entrepreneur *a person who creates and manages a business*

risk *the chance of loss*

Starting a business is hard work. It takes creativity, organizational skills, and courage. It means taking a **risk**. But it can be very rewarding if the business is a success. Many people are happy to run small businesses, and sometimes a small business can grow into a multi-million-dollar company!

Business

Mind Your New Business

Do you have an idea for a business? How are you going to get it up and running? First you'll want to find out if your business has a chance of succeeding. One way to check is by doing a **market survey**. A market survey asks people questions about their likes and dislikes. It asks what goods or services people would use, and how much they'd be willing to pay for them. The answers people give to the survey help business people decide whether or not to move forward with their plans.

This Business Is for the Dogs!

Suppose you wanted to start a dog-walking service. You have the time and you like dogs. But you're not sure if people need this service in your area, and if they do, what specific needs they have. Here's a market survey you could use to find out.

Word Bank
market survey *a questionnaire designed to find out what people think about a particular product or service*

MARKET SURVEY

                                yes no

- Do you have a dog? - - - - - - - - - - - ☐ ☐
- Do you walk your dog more than twice a day? - - - - - - - - - - ☐ ☐
- Are you often too bone-tired to play with your dog? - - - - - - - ☐ ☐
- Does your dog need more exercise? - - ☐ ☐
- Would you pay someone to exercise your dog? - - - - - - - - - - - - - - - ☐ ☐
- Would you pay for this service more than once a week? - - - - - - - - ☐ ☐
- Would you be interested in weekend sessions? - - - - - - - - - - - - - - - ☐ ☐
- Do you know others who would be interested in this service? - - - - - - ☐ ☐

What's the **Plan?**

You started your dog-walking business. After a few weeks, and only a few customers, you panic. You haven't made back the money you spent! Look back. Did you make a business plan? A business plan tells what product or service will be sold and how it will be sold. It tells who the customers will be, how much it will cost to start the business, how much it will cost to run the business, and what the profits are expected to be.

Figuring It All Out

You'll also need a **budget** to work out the financial details of your business. You need to know how many dogs you are going to walk each week and how much to charge each customer. You need to consider how much you are going to spend on advertising. In addition to all these items are your **start-up costs**. Most of these are one-time purchases, such as dog leashes, made before you open your business.

Word Bank

budget *a plan of how much money a person, business, government, or organization has to spend and how it will be spent*

start-up costs *money spent to begin a business*

competition *other businesses selling a similar product*

Sharing the Spotlight

Suppose a friend decides to go into the dog-walking business in your neighborhood, too. You now have **competition**. When you start a business, you have to think about competition. Are there already businesses selling what you want to sell? Where are they? What are their products or services and their prices like? You may have to change your plan altogether.

A Matter of Fact

You might think that a new ice-cream company might not be very successful with all the competition around. Well, with a $12,000 investment ($4,000 of it borrowed), Ben Cohen and Jerry Greenfield opened an ice-cream shop in a renovated gas station in Burlington, Vermont. In 1997, Ben & Jerry's ice cream was sold worldwide, and the company was making a profit of about $6 million a year!

Putting in the Time— and the Money

The market survey is done, the business plan is finished, and you've prepared a budget. But there's still more work to do! You need to contact new customers and make schedules. And you have to actually start walking some dogs! Starting a business is a big **investment**. You may even need to borrow money or have other people invest in your business. This means that they give you money in the hope that when your business is successful, they will get back more money than they invested. Starting a business is a risk, and it's hard work. But just imagine if it's a success!

Keeping Tabs on Your Business

Once your business is off and running, you'll want to check to see how it's doing. You'll need to see if you are making a **profit** or experiencing a **loss**. If your expenses for walking the dogs are more than the money the business has taken in, you'll have a loss. If you have money left over after your business expenses are paid, you've made a profit and can consider yourself a successful entrepreneur!

Business Smarts

Why do some businesses succeed while others fail? Sometimes a business fails due to poor planning or poor management. Sometimes there are other factors. Many people would agree that the secret of success lies not in having the right answers, but rather in asking the right questions, such as *Do people want to buy what I want to sell? Is there any competition for my business? How can I make my business more attractive to customers? Do I have enough money to start the business? How long can I wait before I need to start making a profit?*

A Penny for Your Thoughts

Imagine that there's room for another business in your neighborhood. What kind of business should it be? Ask yourself the questions on the left and find out if you think your business idea would be successful. You might even try to start it up!

Word Bank

investment *the risking of money and time to get something in return*

profit *the money a business earns minus the costs of producing and selling its goods and services*

loss *the money a business loses when the cost of producing its goods and services is greater than the money earned by selling them*

7

Supply and Demand

Is the Price Right?

Ever wonder why certain things cost more than others? It's true that store owners set the prices of their merchandise. But consumers also help determine prices. It's all a matter of **supply** and **demand**—that is, how much people want something and how much of that thing is available. If the demand is greater than the supply, the price goes up. If the supply is greater than the demand, the price goes down. Let's see how that works. Imagine you open a lemonade stand on a cloudy day. You start selling lemonade for 25¢ a glass. You get some customers—not too many, not too few— just enough to make a small profit. Then, the clouds disappear, the sun comes out, and it gets really hot. Now everybody's thirsty! They get in line at your stand. You decide that you can increase your profit if you raise the price to 30¢ a glass. Then you can afford a nicer lemonade stand! People want lemonade because it's hot, so they're willing to pay more. But watch out. If you raise the price too high, people might not want to buy your lemonade at all. What would you pay for a glass of lemonade on a hot day?

A Penny for Your Thoughts

Why do you think people are willing to pay higher prices for diamonds than for water, even though water is a necessity and diamonds aren't?

Not Enough to Go Around

Suppose there are so many people who want lemonade that you don't have enough to go around. Now there is a shortage of lemonade—there are more people who want lemonade than there is lemonade available. You have to go back and forth to the supermarket to buy more ingredients, and that uses up time you could be selling lemonade. You're losing money! You could hire somebody to help you, but that would cost money, too. You think about raising the price to make up the additional costs. If you do, you may be able to make a profit again.

Word Bank

supply *the amount of a good or service that is available to consumers*

demand *the desire of consumers for a good or service*

8

Too Much of a Good Thing

All of a sudden, there's a flash of lightning, a clap of thunder, and within five minutes, it's pouring rain. Suddenly, nobody wants lemonade, because they're running to get out of the rain. There is now a surplus of lemonade. This means that there is more lemonade available than you need for the people who want to buy it. There is a greater supply than demand. You have to lower your price to 10¢ a glass to get anybody to buy some. You hope to at least cover your costs, and you cross your fingers that it won't rain tomorrow! How do you think a lemonade stand would do in a place where it rained a lot?

Making Connections

Did you know that what happens in one part of the marketplace often affects what happens in another? For example, suppose the price of pay TV keeps going down and you could watch any movie at any time. Fewer people might actually go out to the movies. Some theaters might close. What would happen to all that uneaten popcorn? A decreased demand for popcorn at movie theaters could cause a decrease in its price.

Feeling Well—
A Healthy Economy

How do you know if a business is doing well? If there are profits, of course! But an economy doesn't make a profit, so how do you know if the economy is doing well? **Economists**, or people who study the economy, look at lots of different information to see if the economy is healthy. These include the prices of goods and services—whether they are rising or falling—and how many people are out of work or **unemployed**.

Looking for Work?

If you're over 16 and working or looking for work, you're considered part of the nation's work force. But if you're retired or under age 16, you're not counted as part of the work force—even if you do have a job.

The number of unemployed people is very important to the economy. If **unemployment** is low, most people who want a job have one, which usually means the economy is strong. But if the economy is weak, there are fewer jobs so more people have trouble earning money. What happens when unemployment is high? If you said fewer people buy and produce things, you're right.

Word Bank

economist *a person who studies the economy*

unemployed *being without a job, but looking for one*

unemployment *the total number of people out of work*

savings rate *the percent of income that people save*

Savings Rate!

Did you know that saving money can help the economy? For businesses to grow, they need to buy machines, buildings, and other materials. To do this, businesses usually borrow from banks. For money to be available for businesses to borrow, people must deposit savings into their bank accounts. So the **savings rate**—the percent of income that people save—can also tell you about the health of the economy.

A Penny for Your Thoughts

Did you know that the United States' savings rate has declined during the 1980s and 1990s? What do you think Americans are doing with their money instead of saving it?

Economy

Too Much Money?

Would you like to have more money to spend or save? Wouldn't it be great if everyone had more money? It sounds good, but the answer is actually no. When a lot of money is in circulation, **inflation** can occur. When things you buy, either goods or services, cost more than they used to, that's inflation. The prices have increased or inflated. Inflation is another measure of the economy because it shows how well the supply of goods and services in the country are meeting the demand of consumers like you.

Deflating Inflation

Remember how supply and demand affected the lemonade business? The national economy works the same way. If the supply of goods and services is equal to demand, there is little or no inflation. Goods and services cost about the same from year to year. But when there are increases in demand or costs of production go up, prices usually rise.

An increase in demand can be caused by lots of things, including more money in circulation. Why do you think an increase in the money supply increases demand? (Hint: An increase in the money supply means that people have more money and want to spend more on goods and services.)

Word Bank

inflation *an economic condition characterized by rising prices*

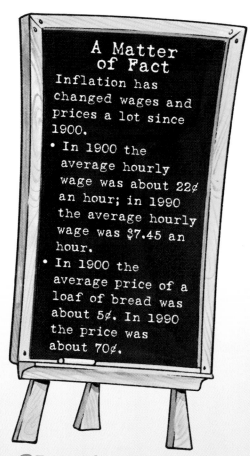

A Matter of Fact

Inflation has changed wages and prices a lot since 1900.

- In 1900 the average hourly wage was about 22¢ an hour; in 1990 the average hourly wage was $7.45 an hour.
- In 1900 the average price of a loaf of bread was about 5¢. In 1990 the price was about 70¢.

Inflation Hurts

Inflation can be hard on people. The value of money goes down during times of inflation. What you buy for a dollar today might cost two dollars tomorrow. This means your money is worth less than it was because it takes twice as much money to buy the same things. In general, many people find that their incomes don't rise as fast as prices.

A recession is when the economy stumbles.

A depression is when the economy trips and falls over!

Downturn or Disaster?

Suppose you're saving to buy a bicycle, but the price of the bicycle is rising faster than you can save. You might decide not to buy the bicycle. What if the same thing happens all across the country? If wages don't increase to keep up with the rising prices, people have less money to spend and products remain unsold. This causes manufacturers to produce fewer products. This leads to a cutback in workers and a rise in unemployment. All of this may cause a **recession**, a short time (two years or less) when the amount of business decreases.

A Penny for Your Thoughts

How well do you think your town's economy is doing? Are prices rising or falling? Are there a lot of jobs available? How can you tell?

Word Bank

recession *a period of time when the demand for goods declines, unemployment rises, and the flow of money slows down*

depression *a period of serious recession marked by high unemployment and a decline in business*

Oh No! A Depression!

Remember when you had a lot of lemonade and no buyers? What do you think would happen if this lasted a long time? Eventually a recession can turn into a **depression**, a time when there are too many goods and services and too little money to buy them. As a result, factories stop producing and shut down. Many people lose their jobs. They have less money or no money to spend. More goods are unsold, more factories close, and more workers are put out of work.

During a depression, prices decline. When there are too many goods for sale, people will sell them for less money rather than not sell them at all. Something that normally costs a dollar may cost only 50 cents. Also, people are willing to work for less money—just to have a job. So it costs less to produce goods.

Depositors waiting for their bank to open, 1930

The Great Depression

The Great Depression began in 1929 and lasted for ten years. In the United States, almost one third of all workers—about 15 million people—were out of work. Some people lost hope that economic conditions would improve, so they withdrew their money from the banks. So many people demanded their money at the same time that the banks couldn't meet their demands. The banks failed and had to close their doors. Millions of people lost their life savings. During the Great Depression 11,000 of the 25,000 banks in the United States closed.

Small Steps Back to Health

How did the United States economy recover? The American people looked to the federal government for help. Measures taken by Presidents Herbert Hoover and Franklin D. Roosevelt restored faith in the economy and provided relief for unemployed workers. Under Roosevelt's New Deal program, the government established the Public Works Administration, which created many new government jobs. As more people became employed, incomes increased and the demand for consumer goods rose as well.

Healthy at Last!

These programs were not enough to end depression conditions completely. The economy did not fully recover until World War II (1941–1945). The war created a demand for workers to not only replace soldiers who were overseas, but to produce the extra food and equipment for the troops. Finally, business improved. The period of **expansion** that everyone had hoped for had arrived.

A Matter of Fact

World War II caused many big changes in the American work force. Many people relocated to places where jobs were more available. Many farmers sold their land. The biggest change was the increase of women in the workplace. Over 5 million women entered the work force.

Word Bank

expansion *a period of time during which the amount of business increases*

13

Take Your Pick!

When Rare Is Well-done!

Old penny stamps are very rare. Today they are worth between $250 and $5,000 each. Ancient coins are very rare, too. People are sometimes willing to pay thousands of dollars for a single silver coin. Why do some things increase in value as they become more scarce? Interview someone who has a stamp or coin collection, and find out what he or she thinks.

The Ups and Downs of Buying Shoes

In January, a new line of sandals came out. In March the price of a pair of the sandals went up $5, as people got ready for warm weather. In July the price rose until the sandals cost twice as much as they did in January. In September the price dropped $8, as summer ended. The September price was $30. How much did the sandals cost in January, March, and July?

A Mower or a Washer?

You're thinking of starting either a lawn-mowing business or a car-washing business. Which one do you think has greater start-up costs? Which one has greater day-to-day expenses? Which one would you rather do?

14

Chapter 2 The Government and Money

Why does the government need money? How does the government get money?

By now, you've probably had experience managing your own money. In this chapter you'll learn how the government manages the country's money.

What is the Federal Reserve System and why do we have it?
What are taxes?
How are our taxes spent?
Why does the government borrow money?

You'll find out a lot about the government and money. You'll see how the Federal Reserve protects the nation's economy. You'll learn about taxes—who pays them and why. You'll learn something about trade around the world. And you'll learn how all this affects you. You're a part of the big picture, and you have a role to play!

Who's in Charge?

The United States is a big country. The American government spends a great deal of money to run the country. So who manages the government's money? It's not the President, it's the Fed! The Federal Reserve System is the government's bank. It is divided into 12 regional banks across the country, with its main headquarters in Washington, D.C. The Fed's main work is to control the amount of money in circulation. It holds a percentage of the deposits of commercial banks and lends money to them when they really need it.

The Federal Reserve is the watchdog of the banking industry. Officials from the Fed regularly check banks' records to make sure they are following banking regulations.

Watchdog — now he's talking my language!

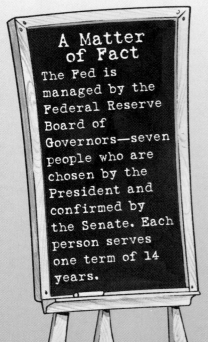

A Matter of Fact

The Fed is managed by the Federal Reserve Board of Governors—seven people who are chosen by the President and confirmed by the Senate. Each person serves one term of 14 years.

What Does the Fed Do?

- controls the amount of money in circulation
- regulates and supervises banks and banking practices
- administers federal consumer credit protection laws, which protect consumers who want credit
- makes sure that there is enough coin and paper money to meet public demand
- handles the government's checking accounts
- buys and sells dollars on foreign exchange markets (You'll learn more about the foreign exchange in the next chapter.)
- processes millions of checks that pass between banks every day

the Head

Controlling the Flow

How does the Fed control the amount of money in circulation? It acts like a traffic cop. When the Fed sees there is too much traffic, or money in the economy, it slows the economy down. The Fed can require banks to put more money in **reserve**—that's money that cannot be loaned. Or the Fed can cause banks to raise the interest rates on loans to customers. The more interest the banks charge, the fewer people want to borrow money. People have less to spend, so the amount of money in circulation decreases.

When there is not enough money in circulation, the Fed allows banks to keep less money in reserve. The banks then have more money to lend and can lower their interest rates to encourage customers to borrow money.

Too Many Dollars

With more money in circulation, people spend more. Businesses expand and hire more people. But sometimes businesses can't produce all the things people want to buy. What happens? Prices may rise. On the other hand, if there isn't enough money in circulation, people won't spend very much. Businesses will not grow, and jobs will be harder to find. It's the Fed's job to keep spending in balance with the production of goods and services. It's quite a balancing act!

Weighing gold at the FRBNY vault

A Penny for Your Thoughts

Suppose prices of goods and services start rising. Would the Fed make credit more or less available? Why?

The Big Guy

The Federal Reserve Bank of New York (FRBNY) is the largest of the 12 Federal Reserve banks. The building has concrete walls 18 feet thick. It also has the largest currency vault in the world and holds 13,000 tons of gold! It is run mostly by computers and robotic devices. These computers and robots work 16 hours a day sorting and counting money. Altogether, the vault processes $2.7 billion a year!

Word Bank

reserve *money that is kept in the bank and not loaned to bank customers*

17

Governments Are

Chipping In by Paying Taxes

Imagine walking down a street. You might see roads, trees, police officers, fire hydrants, schools, garbage cans, and libraries. Did you know that people help pay for all these things? No kidding! People help by paying taxes to city, state, and federal governments. A **tax** is money that a government collects from people and businesses. The government uses taxes to pay for the services it provides, such as schools, libraries, some hospitals, roads and bridges, and the armed forces.

A Penny for Your Thoughts

In France, in the 1600s, more than half of the tax money collected was spent collecting taxes. The cost of collecting taxes in the United States today is 1 percent of the money collected. Why does collecting taxes cost money?

A Pack of Taxes

The government collects taxes in lots of ways. You may pay taxes when you buy certain goods, like books and sports equipment. Adults pay taxes on the money that they earn from their jobs. Companies pay taxes on the profits that they make. People who own buildings pay taxes on the property that the buildings are on. If you inherit money or win the lottery, you pay taxes on what you receive. All the money collected in taxes pays for things that benefit everybody.

How Much Is Just Right?

How does the government decide how much tax people should pay? The government looks at two things: how much money it needs and how much people can afford. The government makes a budget to know how much money it will need to run the country. Then the government must decide how much of this money can be collected in taxes. If the government sets taxes too high, people may have less money to spend. If the government sets taxes too low, it won't be able to take in enough money to meet its expenses. When you're dealing with a multi-billion-dollar budget, it can get a bit tricky!

Did you know your family probably pays more in taxes than it spends on food and clothing combined?

Tax-ing!

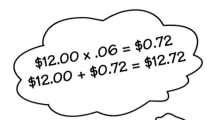

$12.00 × .06 = $0.72
$12.00 + $0.72 = $12.72

Just a Little Bit More

Think about the last time you bought something. You looked at the price tag and thought "Oh, I have to pay that much." But when you got to the counter, the item might have cost a little bit more! That's because you probably paid sales tax on your purchase. **Sales tax** is a **surcharge**, or extra charge, that's sometimes added to specific items, such as clothing and electronic equipment. So suppose you're saving up for a particular item, like a bicycle. Don't forget to save for the sales tax!

Go Figure!

Did you know that you pay more sales tax on a bicycle than you do on a notebook? That's because sales tax is a percent of the total cost of the item. The more an item costs, the greater the sales tax.

Here's how to figure sales tax.

- Find out what the sales tax is in your state. The figure will be a percent, such as 6 percent.

- Change the percent to a decimal. (For example, 6 percent is .06, and 8½ percent is .085.)

- Then multiply that number by the price of the item.

- The product is the correct sales tax. Round off to the nearest penny, if necessary.

- Add the sales tax to the price of the item to get the total amount you have to pay.

$12 plus sales tax

Word Bank

tax *money that one must pay to help support a government*

sales tax *a tax on sales and some services that is usually added to the price by the seller*

surcharge *an extra cost added to an original cost*

19

Putting Your Two Cents In

Did you know that every February, March, and April, adults all over the country are filling out forms? These forms are for their **income tax**, which is a tax that people and businesses pay yearly. Most people pay income tax to state and federal governments. The amount of income tax that people pay is based on their **earned income**—the income they receive through their jobs—and their **unearned income**, such as interest from a savings account and money earned from other investments. Income tax is paid on a certain percent of your income. People who earn more money usually have to pay more taxes than those who earn less. The amount of income tax that people pay also depends on whether they have other people to support, such as children. Do you think the system is fair?

Word Bank

income tax *a tax on a person's income*

earned income *money received from jobs*

unearned income *money received from investments such as savings accounts and bonds*

How Much Would You Pay?

Do you earn any money? If it's less than $4,000 a year, you don't have to pay income tax. But suppose you had a full-time job. How much you earn determines the percent you have to pay. Look at the chart and you'll see!

Federal Income Tax for a Single Person, 1997

If Income Is	Percent Taken Out
less than $24,000	15%
$24,000 to $58,150	28%
$58,150 to $121,300	31%
$121,300 to $263,750	36%
more than $263,750	39.6%

A Do-It-Yourself Income Tax

What do you think about having a family income tax? Here's how it would work. Each member of the family must contribute a percent of his or her total income or allowance weekly into a large jar or container—known as the tax jar. At the end of the year, decide together what to do with the money. Will you put it toward a family trip? Will you go out for dinner? Will you buy a computer game?

Who Pays Taxes?

Is everybody chipping in? Yes, everyone who lives and works in the United States must pay income taxes. But there are a few exceptions. For instance, people who visit the United States from other countries and stay and work for a short time do not pay income tax. These individuals are **tax-exempt**, which means they do not have to pay taxes on their income.

Like individuals, certain organizations are tax-exempt. **Nonprofit** groups, such as colleges, churches, and charitable organizations, are excused from paying taxes. A nonprofit organization is one that uses all the money it makes to cover its expenses and to further its goals. For instance, a religious institution such as a church uses the money it makes to pay for its programs and employees and to create more programs.

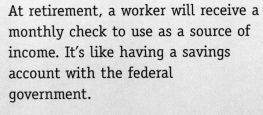

A Penny for Your Thoughts

Can you think of any ideas for a nonprofit organization? Are there any causes that you would like to work on? Do you know of any nonprofit organizations that work for that cause?

Looking to the Future

Ever wonder how people pay for things after they retire? In addition to retirement savings, investments, or other income, many people receive **Social Security** benefits. Social Security is a federal system of financial support for retired workers and people who are unable to work because of a disability. Workers pay into the system by having Social Security taxes deducted from their pay. Employers are also required to pay taxes to Social Security for each employee. At retirement, a worker will receive a monthly check to use as a source of income. It's like having a savings account with the federal government.

Word Bank

tax-exempt *excused from paying taxes*

nonprofit *not intending to make a profit*

Social Security *a system of government financial support for those who are retired or unable to work*

SOCIAL SECURITY

999 12 3456

THIS NUMBER HAS BEEN ESTABLISHED FOR

Lynn Evans
SIGNATURE

Even the Government

When Taxes Aren't Enough

What do you do when you need something right away but don't have the money to pay for it? You might borrow money from your family or from a friend. When the federal or state government needs money, it does the same thing—it borrows money! But the government doesn't go to the bank to get a loan. Instead it sells certificates called **bonds**. A bond is like a loan to the government or any large company. And just like a bank loan, the borrower must pay interest to the lender. And who is the lender? It could be you! Is buying government bonds a safe investment? Yes! If the government doesn't have enough money to pay off its bonds, it can issue new bonds or raise taxes.

It's a Bond-ing Experience

Though the government issues many different bonds, the most common ones are savings bonds. Where do you get them? What do they cost? You can buy a savings bond at most banks or from a Federal Reserve bank. Your cost or investment is half the face value. That means if you buy a $50 bond, it will cost you $25. It will be worth the face value or $50 when the bond **matures**, which could be in 10 years. But you can cash in the bond at any time after 6 months. Just remember, the longer you hold a bond, the more interest it earns.

A Matter of Fact

The government issues several different types of savings bonds. They may be bought in denominations of $50, $100, $500, $1,000, $5,000, and $10,000.

Word Bank

bond *a certificate of a loan to a government or business*

mature *able to be redeemed for the face value*

Borrows Money

Government Overspending

Do you owe anybody any money? If you do, you and the federal government have something in common. Over the years, the federal government has spent a lot of money. It has also run up a huge **debt**. The **national debt** is more than $5 trillion ($5,000,000,000,000). Now that's a lot of zeros! If this debt were divided among every man, woman, and child in the United States, each person would owe about $20,000. How did the government build up so much debt? As you can see from the chart, it took a lot of time. Often the cost of war causes a big increase in the national debt. It all started when the government took over $75 million in debts accumulated from the Revolutionary War.

The interest owed on the national debt is over $300,000,000!

That's going to keep everybody interest-ed for a long time! That's more than $821,917 a day!

We've Got a Big Debt

What happens if you owe a lot of money to a lot of people? For one thing, you have to work extra hard to pay off the debt. If everybody that you owe money to wanted it at one time, you'd be in a jam. Also, if you owe too much money, people may stop lending you money. What about the government's debt? To pay off the debt, the government might raise taxes. When taxes are raised, people have less money to spend. Less money spent means less business growth and fewer new jobs. And it's possible that if the debt continues to grow, people may stop lending money to the government.

National Debt

Year	Amount of Debt
1800	$82,976,294
1825	$83,788,433
1850	$63,452,774
1875	$2,232,284,532
1900	$2,136,961,091
1925	$20,516,193,888
1950	$257,357,352,351
1975	$576,649,000,000*
1995	$4,921,018,000,000*

*Rounded to millions

Word Bank

debt *the money owed when you buy something on credit or borrow money*

national debt *the amount of money the government owes*

23

Money All Over

Money Makes the World Go Round

When you buy something at the supermarket, what do you use? Dollars and cents of course! You may pay with cash, credit cards, or checks, but it's still in dollars and cents. The dollar is the main unit of currency in the United States. If everyone in the world used the same currency, life would be simple. But each country has its own money. In fact, there are approximately 140 different currencies in the world today.

Import or Export?

What kinds of products are made where you live? Every country produces different types of products. One country must trade with another to get products that are not produced within its own country. Goods that are brought into a country for sale from other countries are called **imports**. Goods that a country sends to other countries for sale are called **exports**. What goods are imported into the United States? Can you think of any goods that we export?

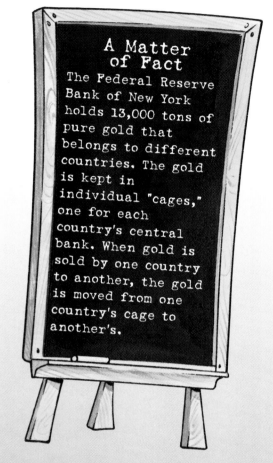

A Matter of Fact
The Federal Reserve Bank of New York holds 13,000 tons of pure gold that belongs to different countries. The gold is kept in individual "cages," one for each country's central bank. When gold is sold by one country to another, the gold is moved from one country's cage to another's.

A Dollar, A Pound

If you visit another country and buy something, you usually have to pay for the item with that country's money. To do this, you would exchange your money for the currency of the country you are in. But the value of currency in each country might be different. For instance, one British pound may be worth two American dollars. If this were true, which would you rather have, one pound or one dollar?

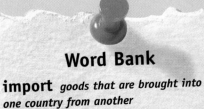

Word Bank

import *goods that are brought into one country from another*

export *goods that are sent from one country to another*

24

the World

The Foreign Exchange Market

How do you think the value of currencies are agreed upon? How much a currency is worth compared to another currency, called the **exchange rate**, is determined at the **foreign exchange market**. This is the place where foreign exchange dealers in major cities like New York, London, Tokyo, and Paris trade the money of different countries.

Currency Exchange Board

			We Sell At	We Buy At
●	CANADA	CAD	888.928	86.839
●	UNITED KINGDOM	GBP	888.884	881.703
●	JAPAN	YEN	8.00812	.00733
●	SWITZERLAND	SFR	888.786	888.665
●	FRANCE	FRF	888.199	888.173
●	W. GERMANY	DEM	488.668	888.690
●	AUSTRALIA	A$	8.8720	.7550
●	SPAIN	PTS	8.01026	.00950
●	ITALY	LIRE	000855	000801

How Does It Work?

How are exchange rates determined? They are based on supply and demand. For example, if Americans want to buy Japanese goods, they need Japanese money, or yen, to pay for the goods. This creates a demand for the yen, so the value of the yen goes up. When the value of the yen goes up, Japanese goods become more expensive. If the goods become too expensive, people will buy fewer Japanese goods. Then the value of the yen will fall. And people will be able to get more yen for a dollar.

Word Bank

exchange rate *the value of one nation's currency in comparison to another*

foreign exchange market *the place where foreign exchange dealers in major cities around the world trade the money of different countries*

A Test of Strength

Did you know that the dollar can be weak or strong? When the dollar has a high value in comparison with the currencies of other countries, it is considered strong. This happens when there is a large demand for American goods. On the other hand, when the demand for American goods and services is low, the dollar is weak—it has a low value compared with the currencies of other countries. When you travel abroad, you will be able to buy more with your money if the dollar is strong.

A Penny for Your Thoughts

Suppose you have a choice between something made in America or something that has been imported. What are some reasons you might choose one over the other?

25

Take Your Pick!

Taxing Questions

If there were no taxes, would there be public schools? Is there anything else that would be missing from your community if there were no taxes? Suppose your state wanted to build a bridge. How could it get the money?

Buy Time

You just received $35 for your birthday. You want to buy a new jacket for $32.99, but the sales tax is 8 percent. Do you have enough money?

Currency Exchange Rates

Where can you get the best buy? Suppose the same bicycle costs 200 American dollars, 130 British pounds, 417 German marks, and 22,542 Japanese yen. Look in the newspaper to find the current exchange rates for these currencies. Where can you get the best deal?

It's Import-ant!

Are you wearing an import? Perhaps your shoes were made in another country. How do you think they got to your feet? Make up a story describing "The Great Traveling Shoes."

Chapter 3

Investing
Money

Why should I **invest?**
What are my **options?**

You've learned the importance of saving money and spending it wisely. In this chapter, you will learn that sometimes you can really make the money you save grow.

What are stocks and bonds?
What's so great about the stock market?
What does it mean to invest money wisely?

This chapter will help you understand the ins and outs of owning stock. You'll learn how the stock market works. You'll understand the difference between stocks and bonds. You'll learn that there are different ways to invest your money. When it comes to money, you won't be green anymore!

Stocking Up

It's in Stock!

Suppose you own a small business, such as a lawn-mowing service. But you don't have enough money to buy the new lawn mower you need. What could you do to get more money? You could borrow money or you could invite friends to share in the cost of your business—for a profit of course.

This is similar to what companies do when they need money to expand or grow. They sell stock. **Stocks** are like bricks in a building. If you own a brick, you own a **share**, or part of the building. Owning a stock means that you are a **stockholder** or a **shareholder**—a part owner of the company. So you own a share of everything the company owns.

Opening Up to Stockholders

When the owners of a company decide they want to sell stock in their company, they "go public." This means they sell shares to anyone who wants to buy them. How many shares do they sell? It's up to the owners of the company. It could be one hundred, one thousand, one million, or more.

A Penny for Your Thoughts

If you owned shares in a company that made cars, what might you want the company to focus on? New models, cutting costs, new technology?

Having a Say in the Company

Congratulations! You've bought stock! When you hold stock in a company, you can have a say in how the company is run. Every year, shareholders are invited to an annual shareholders' meeting. At the meeting they may vote on certain future company plans. Every share is worth one vote. As you might have guessed, the more shares a person has, the more power he or she has in company decision-making.

A stock certificate

Word Bank

stock *a part of a company that may be purchased by the public*

share *a part of a company that may be bought by someone as an investment*

stockholder or shareholder *a person who owns stock or shares in a company*

on Stocks

A Matter of Fact

In the game of poker, plastic chips are used to represent money. The most valuable chips in the game are blue. So *blue-chip stocks* has come to mean the most valuable stocks— they cost more—but have very little chance of losing their value. Some blue-chip stocks are Coca Cola, IBM, General Motors, and Pepsi.

It Can Be Good to Stock Up

Why do people buy stock? To make money! You want your stock to be worth more than what you paid. If the company does well, you can expect the value of your shares to go up. If you decided to sell your shares, you would receive more money than you paid. You can hold onto your shares for as long as you want. You choose when you want to sell them. You may also receive **dividends**, which are part of the company's profits. Some of the profits are divided among the stockholders, who usually receive dividends every three months.

Good Times and Bad

What happens if the company that you own stock in has a loss? The value of your shares would probably go down. Investing in stocks can be tricky! As part owner of the company, you must take the good times with the bad. There is always the risk that the value of the shares you buy will go down. It is possible that the value of your shares can go down so far that you lose the money you invested in the company. So before you buy stock in a company, you should do some research. What does the company do? How long has it been around? Has it been successful?

Word Bank
dividend *a share of the profits received by a stockholder*

The Supermarket

Who's Selling?

You've done your research, and you've decided to invest some money in a particular company. Where do you go? When you want to buy or sell stocks, you contact a **stockbroker,** a person who buys and sells shares of stock for customers. Stockbrokers are paid **commissions**, or fees, on the stocks they buy and sell. A commission is usually a percent of the total cost of the stocks bought or sold.

This is Some Market!

If you ever listen to news reports on TV or radio, you might have heard about stocks rising and falling. What does that mean? The prices are going up or going down. Prices of stocks are determined by the **stock market**, where they are bought and sold. Stock prices may change daily. The stock market is like a supermarket for buying and selling shares in different companies. If there are many people who want to buy a share in a company, the price of the shares will go up. If there are many people who want to sell shares in a company, the price will go down.

The Big Board

The United States stock market is made up of several different stock exchanges or stock markets. The three main ones are the New York Stock Exchange (NYSE), the National Association of Securities Dealers Automated Quotations (NASDAQ) exchange, and the American Stock Exchange (AMEX). NYSE and AMEX are located in New York City. But NASDAQ is actually a system of computers that are networked, or linked together.

Did you know that 51 million Americans own stock?

A Penny for Your Thoughts

Do you think buying stocks is a good investment? Would you rather buy stock or keep your money in a savings account? Why?

Word Bank

stockbroker *a person who buys and sells shares of stock for other people*

commission *the fee paid to a stockbroker for buying or selling stocks*

stock market *a place where shares of many different companies are bought and sold*

# of Stocks

If you've ever seen stockbrokers in action, buying and selling stocks at the New York Stock Exchange, you'd think you were in the middle of a giant rush-hour traffic jam. The place is crowded and noisy. People rush back and forth. It's quite different from the early days of the NYSE. In 1792, 24 brokers and merchants met under a tree on Wall Street in New York City.

Bulls and Bears

At the original New York Stock Exchange, people put notes on a bulletin board when they wanted to buy or sell stocks. When the market was doing well, there were many notes or "bulletins" on the board. When the market wasn't doing well, the board was bare. Today a market in which stocks are rising is called a **bull market**. "Bulls" are people who expect stock prices to rise. A market in which stock prices are falling is called a **bear market**. "Bears" are people who expect stock prices to drop. Is today's market bullish or bearish? Look in the newspaper or listen to the news to find out!

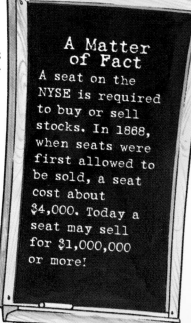

If we're in a bear market, I guess things could get a bit hairy!

A Matter of Fact
A seat on the NYSE is required to buy or sell stocks. In 1868, when seats were first allowed to be sold, a seat cost about $4,000. Today a seat may sell for $1,000,000 or more!

The New York Stock Exchange

Word Bank
bull market *a period in which the stock market does well and prices are up*

bear market *a period in which the stock market does poorly and prices go down*

31

Boning Up on the Stock Market

Suppose you saved up some money and bought 10 shares of Reebok stock. The value of your stock may change every day. Your stock may go up while other stocks are going down. To find out the value of your stock, turn to the business section of a newspaper or search the Internet to find the stock report or quote. A stock report looks much more complicated than it actually is. Here's a close-up of one from a newspaper.

NEW YORK STOCK EXCHANGE COMPOSITE TRANSACTIONS

Stock — the company's name or logo

Volume — the number of shares that were bought and sold during the day

Dividend — the portion of the profits paid to stockholders

P/E (price earnings) a ratio determined by dividing the current price of a share of stock by the earnings per share

Stock
Reebok

Ticker Symbol
RBK

Close
$39^{5/16}$

Volume
99,800

52-Week High/Low
$34/52^{7/8}$

Dividend
.75

EPS
2.0

P/E
11

Ticker Symbol — a three- to five-letter "code," the official symbol stockbrokers use to identify the stock

Close — the last price paid per share

52-Week High/Low — the highest and lowest prices of the stock in the last year

EPS (earnings per share) a company's profits over the past year divided by the number of shares

STOCK QUOTES

32

A Penny for Your Thoughts

What kind of things would you look for in a stock investment?

Winning on Wall Street

Is there any way to really know if stocks will go up or down? Not really. The best advice about choosing stocks, however, is to follow three simple steps.

STEP 1 Buy stock in a company you know something about. We all have to eat and take medicine, even when there may be less money than usual to spend. Food and drug stocks, therefore, are safe bets since they tend to hold their prices even during troubled times. Other industries that remain pretty steady are gas, water, electric, and phone companies.

STEP 2 Research a few companies. Call a brokerage firm and ask for information on the companies you've chosen. Follow the stocks' prices in the newspaper or on-line. Call the companies and ask for their annual reports.

So Who Is This Guy?

Have you ever heard of Dow Jones? Dow Jones & Company is a financial news publisher that researches the stock market. This research is used by investors to help predict when stocks will increase or decrease in value. The **Dow Jones Industrial Average,** also called the Dow, is a number that indicates the average of closing prices of 30 selected stocks. These stocks are chosen because their performance is a good indicator of how the stock market is doing overall. If the Dow is rising, the rest of the stock market is generally rising, too. Take a look in the newspaper. Did the Dow rise or fall yesterday?

STEP 3 Know your investment goals. Do you want your money to grow to meet a future need, such as college? Or do you want income to spend right now? How much risk are you willing to take? Identifying your goals will help you determine which stock to buy.

Word Bank

Dow Jones Industrial Average (DJIA)
a number indicating the average closing prices of the 30 industrial stocks; also called the Dow

So Many Ways to Invest

Have you ever looked in the financial section of the newspaper or listened to the financial news on TV? There's a lot more to the world of big business than stocks. You have many options, or choices for investing. Armed with that knowledge, one day you'll be ready to take on the world of investing!

These Bonds Don't Break

Remember, one way the government borrows money is by selling bonds. Well, companies can sell bonds, too. These bonds allow you to invest money for a fixed period of time at a fixed interest rate. You receive interest regularly until the bond matures. Once it does, you receive the principal back.

Is a fixed interest rate a good thing? It can be good or bad. Suppose that, after you buy a bond, the interest rates on new bonds change. If the bond you bought has an interest rate of 12 percent and interest rates on new bonds are lower, your bond becomes more valuable. If the interest rate on new bonds is higher, your bond becomes less valuable.

Stocks or Bonds?

What's the difference between stocks and bonds? When you buy stock, you are buying a share in a company. But when you buy bonds, you are just lending money to the company. You don't have a say in the way the company is run. And no matter how the company does, you still receive the same amount of interest.

A Penny for Your Thoughts

Would you rather buy stocks or bonds? Would you rather buy government bonds or company bonds?

Options?

Having a Fund Time

Suppose you bought several shares of stock from a few different companies. Your investments did well. Now your friends ask if you would invest some money for them. This is similar to how a **mutual fund** works. A mutual fund is a company that sells stock in itself to investors and then uses that money to invest in other companies. The fund is run by a professional manager. It is up to the professional, not the individual investors, to decide what to buy and sell. Since a mutual fund has a variety of different investments, its success does not depend on one particular stock or bond. Why might you invest in a mutual fund? Maybe you don't feel confident about buying stocks or bonds by yourself. Maybe you don't have the time or knowledge to follow the stock market and make informed choices. Also, the fact that the fund has many customers like yourself enables the fund to have more power in making investments.

There's Still More!

Did you know that there are many more ways to invest your money? You can buy real estate (houses, buildings, and land). You can buy precious gems and metals, such as diamonds and gold. You can invest in foreign currencies or in natural resources like oil. You can put money into small businesses that are just starting. You can invest money in your own small business! You have many options.

Word Bank

mutual fund *a company that sells stock in itself and then uses that money to invest in other companies*

35

Balancing Risk

Hey, Big Spender!

Suppose you had $5,000. What would you do with it?

When you save or invest money, you must think about how much risk you are willing to take. The safer your investment, the less money you are likely to earn. The riskier the investment, the greater the chance you have of losing your money or making a lot of money.

Each type of investment, from stocks to bonds to mutual funds, has a certain amount of risk. In general, the riskier an investment, the greater the possible profit. When you choose investments, you have to decide how much risk you want to take. The risk you are willing to take depends on what your goals are, your personality, and how much time and money you are willing to invest.

Word Bank

portfolio *a collection of investments, such as stocks, bonds, and bank accounts*

Keeping It in Mind

How should you weigh risk and return? First of all, you have to decide why you are investing. Do you want an income now, or are you saving for something further down the road? The longer the period you invest your money for, the less the ups and downs of the stock market will affect you. So the risk is less. You also have to decide how much risk you can handle. If you take a big risk with your money, will you spend lots of sleepless nights worrying if your investments are doing well? Everybody has a certain level of risk that they feel comfortable taking. You may want to make a lot of money, but if you're worrying all the time, the risk is probably not worth it.

Putting It All Together

Do you think you should put all your money into one investment? Many people invest their money in a variety of ways. They buy some stocks and some bonds and also deposit money in a bank account. Your **portfolio** consists of all the investment choices that you have made. The contents of your portfolio are up to you, depending on your needs and goals.

A Matter of Fact
Americans invest more money in bonds than in stocks or mutual funds.

and Reward

Investment Choices

Each type of investment has its own level of risk. Which suits your needs best?

Bank accounts Bank accounts, like savings accounts, CDs, and money market accounts, have a very small amount of risk. But these accounts pay relatively low rates of interest.

Bonds Bonds are usually a safe investment. But be careful whose bonds you buy. Sometimes bonds that pay higher interest rates are riskier because the company that issued them may not be able to pay you when the bond is due. In general, government bonds are the safest.

Mutual funds The risk of investing in a mutual fund depends on the kinds of stocks and bonds it buys. For example, a mutual fund that invests in blue-chip stocks and bonds is much less risky than a mutual fund that invests in new technology stocks.

Stocks Buying individual stocks can be very rewarding but also very risky. You have to know what you're doing.

A Penny for Your Thoughts

So now you know something about investing money. What tips do you have to share with others? What are things to consider? What are things to avoid?

When the Payoff's Not Cash

You can put money to work for you in many ways. But money can also be shared with others to help those who are in need. How you choose to donate your time or money toward helping others is a personal matter. Some people donate money to support particular causes, such as protecting the environment. Others donate money to organizations like UNICEF, which helps needy children by providing food, medicine, and education programs. Understanding how to use money—to benefit yourself and others—is an important life skill. You now have a lot of the know-how in your pocket. How you choose to use it to build a productive and rewarding life is up to you.

Take Your Pick!

It's a Zoo!

Here are some terms that have to do with the stock market. Can you guess how they got their names?

cage—the room in the broker's office where cash and securities are handled

cash cow—a company that earns a lot of money

cats and dogs—poor-quality stocks

goldbugs—investors who think that buying gold is the best investment

turkey—a poor investment; a dud

Keeping a Close Eye on Your Investments

Choose a stock to follow. It could be the company that makes your favorite sneakers, movies, toys, cereal—you name it! Check the newspaper's business section to see if the company is publicly traded on a stock exchange. Then you can see how "your company" is doing every day. Would your company be a good investment?

Buy Low, Sell High

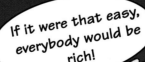

Buying stock is a cinch. You buy low and sell high. That means buy stock when the price is low and sell stock when the price is high.

If it were that easy, everybody would be rich!

Why do you think investing in stock is not as easy as she says it is?